Life in the UK Citizenship Test:

Ultimate Revision Guide 2017

Acknowledgements

A big thank you to everyone who has provided feedback to enable us to improve our publications.

.

Neepradaka Press

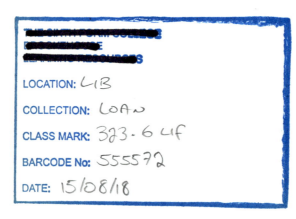

Contents

Introduction

Anyone applying for Indefinite leave to remain (settlement) or British Citizenship, are required to sit a 45 minute multiple choice test called, the 'Life in the UK test'. The Home Office provides official study materials to help prepare for the test.

However, many people have found these materials quite difficult to use in their preparations. Some have tried other publications which claim to help you study for the test, however again these have proved to be ineffective.

This book attempts to solve these problems by simplifying ideas and concepts, and setting out the material in a way which will allow maximum absorption and retention, and to allow everyone to take the Life in the UK Test with full confidence.

Before you start

It is essential that you read through the official Life in the UK test material published by the Home Office before you use this book. By doing so you will be able to get a wide overview of the material that you will need to learn. We would recommend reading through the official book at least three times, after which you will be ready to make use of this book.

How to use this book

We recommend that you spend a week on each chapter of this book. Read through one chapter as many times as you can. Then take small sections of text and make sure you understand the concepts and ideas presented.

The text has been specifically arranged in a way which makes concepts and ideas easy to understand, and includes key words which will come up in the test, trigger your memory, and allow you to answer the questions correctly. This is based on the latest brain research and how memory works.

Once you have spent a week on each chapter, go back and read through the Official Life in the UK test book. There will be names of particular people, and other bits of information which have been deliberately omitted from this book. You will find it much easier to add extra names and information from the Home Office book to your memory, as it will have a strong memory framework to attach to.

Finally, we would encourage you to try practice questions which will indicate you how much you have been able to remember and understand. If there are questions you have difficulty on, then you will be able to refer back to this book and revise those particular concepts.

The book has been tested by thousands of users, and was revised and edited following their feedback. We would welcome further feedback and will be able to use this for future editions. Please send feedback via the publishers to: admin@neepradaka.co.uk

Good Luck!

Chapter 1: A long and illustrious society

Early Britain

First people were hunter gatherers who moved to Britain in the Stone Age.

First farmers arrived 6,000 years ago: built tombs, houses and monuments (Stone Henge in Wiltshire is one such monument).
Skara Brae in Orkney: is the best preserved prehistoric village.

4,000 years ago: the bronze age-: the people were skilled in metalwork, and made gold, tools and weapons.

Iron age: Iron was used to make tools and weapons. People lived in roundhouses. They defended hill forts against invaders. Celtic was the main language. Coins were first to be minted at this time, with the names of Iron age Kings.

The Romans

Julius Caesar invaded Britain in 55 BC but was defeated.
Emperor Claudius invaded later.
Boudicca: she was from the Iceni tribe who fought against the Romans. Her statue is at Westminster Bridge near House of Parliament.

Anglo-Saxon's

Brought the English language in to Britain.

Anglo-Saxon King is buried at Sutton hoo, which is in Suffolk. He was buried with his ship and treasure.

Missionaries came to Britain to teach Christianity. The most famous was Saint Patrick who became the Patron Saint of Ireland.

Saint Columba: founded a monastery in Scotland.

Saint Augustine from Rome, became first Archbishop of Canterbury.

Vikings

They came from Denmark and Norway.

Anglo-Saxon Kingdoms joined together under King Alfred the Great to fight the Vikings and win.

Some Vikings stayed and mixed with others. King Canute was a Danish King. In the North, people united under King Kenneth MacAlpin. Scotland began to be used to describe the North.

Norman Conquest

1066: William Duke of Normandy defeats Harold at the battle of Hastings, and is known as William the conqueror.

The battle is shown on Bayeux Tapestry (embroidery on cloth). It survives to this day, and can be seen in France.

Domesday book: William sent people to make a list of towns, villages, people, and what they owned. Book can still be seen today.

Middle Ages

After the Norman Conquest, up to 1485 is known as middle ages (medieval period): this was a time of constant war.

King Edward I in 1284 introduces the Statute of Rhuddlan 1284- this meant Wales became part of England.

4

Robert the Bruce (Scottish), defeats the English at battle of Bannockburn. In Ireland: the English ruled a small part called the Pale (around Dublin).

The Crusades: Knights fought for control of Holy land.

Hundred Years war: English Kings fight France for 116 years. A famous Battle is called the Battle of Agincourt 1415.

Feudalism and the Black Death

Feudalism: Kings gave land to Lords. Land was worked on by Serfs. Serfs could grow food for themselves, but had to work for their Lord and could not move anywhere else.

1348: Plague came to Britain. Many died. Shortage of labour meant that peasants could demand higher wages. More people left the countryside to live in towns.

Legal/political changes

The King had advisors: these were leaders of church, and noblemen. There were few limits to the King's power.
Noblemen forced King John to agree to demands. This was called charter of rights or Magna Carta.
In the future the King had to involve noblemen in his decisions. The King would hold Parliaments to allow discussions to take place.

Two parts or houses developed. One part which was the noblemen and bishops was known as 'House of Lords'. Another part were small landowners and wealthy people- this part was called the 'House of Commons'.

In Scotland there were three houses: Lords, commons and clergy.

Legal system: Judges were established and were independent of Government. Judges developed common law. The process was called precedence (following previous decisions).

In Scotland laws were codified (written down).

Distinct identity

Middle ages saw the development of National culture and identity.

English language is born (mix of Anglo-Saxon and French Norman).

1400: Geoffrey Chaucer wrote 'The Canterbury Tales'. His book was first to be printed by William Caxton (he used the printing press to print many books).

In Scotland, John Barbour wrote 'The Bruce' which was about the battle of Bannockburn. He wrote in the Scots language.

Castles were built in many places. Great cathedrals like Lincoln cathedral were built. They had stained glass windows. The glass in York Minster is a famous example.

Wool was an important export.

People came from abroad to trade, work, and brought with them special skills.

War of roses: Two families: Houses York (symbol of a white rose), and House of Lancaster (symbol of red rose), were at War with each other. When King Henry married King Richard's niece, both houses joined together. They became House of Tudor (red and white rose joined).

Tudors and Stuarts

Religious conflict

Henry VIII: He broke away from the Roman church to divorce his first wife because the Pope (Catholic), would not give permission to divorce.

Henry established his own church, and appointed bishops. This was called the 'Church of England'. Wales united with England.

In Europe there began the start of a reformation: movement against the authority of the Pope. People wanted thier own church, and for the Bible reading to be in thier own language, and stop praying to saints.

In Ireland, an attempt to impose Protestantism failed.

When Henry VIII dies, his son Edward becomes King at age 9. He died age 15, and half sister Mary became Queen (Catholic). She was known as 'Bloody Mary' for persecuting Protestants.

After Mary dies, her half-sister Elizabeth is Queen (Protestant). She avoided conflict by not asking people about their real religious beliefs.

Spanish Armada: ships were sent by Spain to restore Catholicism. Sir Francis was commander of English ship. His ship 'Golden Hind', sailed around the world (circumnavigated).

Elizabethan Period: was a time of growing pride in being English.

Development of poetry/drama

William Shakespeare: born Stratford-upon-Avon. Wrote plays and poems. Famous plays are 'Hamlet' and 'Romeo and Juliet'.

After Elizabeth, cousin James VI (of Scotland) becomes James I, King of England. He introduces a new translation of the Bible called the 'King James Version', and it is still used today.

Ireland

Majority of Ireland was still Catholic, but England tried to settle and take over Catholic land.

Rise of parliament

James and his son Charles believed in the divine right of Kings (do what they wanted without consulting or getting approval from Parliament). When Charles tried to impose his prayer book in Scotland, a Scottish army was formed against him.

Charles asked Parliament for money for army to fight, but Parliament refused.

In Ireland, another rebellion was taking place, and Parliament tried to take control of the army. Charles I entered Parliament to arrest leaders but they had been been warned, and so were not there.

So a civil war started in 1642 between the Kings Army (Cavaliers), and Parliament supporters (Roundheads). Charles lost and was killed 1649.

England becomes a republic-called commonwealth.

Oliver Cromwell

Army was in control. One of its generals, Oliver Cromwell, was sent to Ireland, where revolt had begun in 1641. Cromwell was successful in establishing the authority of the English Parliament.

Cromwell was recognised as the leader of the new republic, and given title of Lord Protector, and he ruled until his death in 1658.

When Cromwell died, his son, Richard, became Lord Protector, but was not able to control the army or the government.

Britain had been a republic for 11 years, but without Oliver Cromwell there was no clear leader or system of government.

Many people in the country wanted stability.

The Restoration

Parliament invited Charles II to come back from exile in the Netherlands. He was crowned King Charles II of England, Wales, Scotland and Ireland.

The Church of England again became the established official Church. Both Roman Catholics and Puritans were kept out of power.

1665: A major outbreak of plague in London. Thousands of people die, especially in poorer areas.

1666: Great fire of London destroys much of the city, including many churches and St Paul's Cathedral. London was rebuilt with a new St Paul's Cathedral, designed by a famous architect, Sir Christopher Wren.

Samuel Pepys wrote about these events in a diary, which was later published and is still read today.

1679: The Habeas Corpus Act became law. No one could be held prisoner unlawfully. Every prisoner has a right to a court hearing.

Charles II was interested in science and the 'Royal Society' was formed to promote 'natural knowledge'. It is the oldest surviving scientific society in the world. Early members were:

Sir Edmund Halley: predicted the return of the comet which is now called Halley's Comet.

Sir Isaac Newton: Law of Gravity, discovered white light is made up of colours of the rainbow.

A Catholic King

Charles II had no children. Brother King James (Catholic) becomes King. James arrested bishops. People were worried that James wanted to make England Catholic. He had two protestant daughters (one called Mary). His wife later had a boy.

Glorious Revolution

James's daughter Mary (married to William of Orange), was asked by Protestants to invade England and become a (Protestant) King.

James ran away, and William became King William III. He ruled with wife Mary.

James tried to invade Ireland and William defeated him at the Battle of Boyne. James escaped to France.

Scotland supported James. But a rebellion was defeated at Killiecrankie. Scottish clans had to support William as King.

When William and Mary were crowned, a declaration of rights was read.

A Global Power

Constitutional monarchy-bill of rights

Bill of rights. A declaration at the Coronation which confirmed rights of Parliament and the limits of the King's power.

Parliament controlled who could be Monarch, and that they had to be Protestant. Parliament was elected every 3 years (later 7 then 5). This meant a Monarch had to ask Parliament to renew funding for the army and navy.

1695: newspapers did not need a government license.

After William III, ministers became more important.

Only men with property of high value could vote. Some places had no voters (rotten borough's). Some places had mostly wealthy families living there (pocket borough's).

People were leaving Britain and Ireland to settle in America and elsewhere.

1680 & 1720: refugees (Huguenots) arrived who had been persecuted as Protestants. Many were educated and were skilled bankers and scientists, as well skilled in weaving or other crafts.

Act or treaty of union in Scotland

William and Mary successors was Queen Anne.
Queen Anne had no surviving children. Parliament chose a German protestant (nearest protestant relative) to be King.

Prime Minister

German King spoke little English so he had a 'Prime Minister' to help and advise him. He was called Sir Robert Walpole.

Robert Burns

A Scottish poet. Wrote in Scots language (English with Scottish words). His song is sung at Hogmanay (New Years Eve festival in Scotland).

The Enlightenment

18th century. New ideas about politics, philosophy, and science developed.

Some notable people are:

Adam Smith: economics.

David Hume: philosopher-human nature.

James Watt: steam power (this progressed the industrial revolution).

Most important principle: everyone has right to their own political or religious belief and state should not dictate them.

Industrial revolution

Before 18th century, agriculture was the biggest employment.

People worked at home to produce goods.

After 18th century steam power & machinery developed and this was called the 'industrial revolution'.

Agriculture and manufacturing became mechanized.

Coal was needed to power machinery. People moved to work in mines or in factories.

Bessemer process: this process enabled the mass production of steel. This meant that ships and railways could develop rapidly.

Richard Arkwright: was barber, made wigs, then worked in textiles. Improved the carding machine, which prepared fibres for spinning in to yarn & fabric.

Transport was needed to move goods. Canals were built to link factories towns and cities to shipping ports.

Working conditions were poor during industrial revolution. Children worked and treated harshly.

Colonization abroad increased, Britain took control over parts of the world.

East India company: was first setup to trade in India, and then took over parts of India.

Sake Dean Mahomet

From Bengal. Moved to Ireland. Eloped with an Irish girl. Set up a Coffee house. Made curry. His wife introduced shampoo.

Slave trade

Slavery was illegal in Britain, but was established in overseas industry (British and American colonies were there). Slaves travelled on British ships in bad conditions, and treated badly. Slaves were taken to the Caribbean to work on tobacco and sugar plantations.

In Britain there were people trying to stop slavery such as the Quakers, and a man called William Wilberforce (a Member of Parliament). He succeeded in turning public opinion against slavery.

1807: Illegal to trade slaves in British ships ports.
1833: Emancipation act- abolished slavery throughout British Empire.
After 1833: two million Indian and Chinese workers replaced slaves.

American War of Independence

British colony in North Americas wanted control of their own affairs. British wanted to tax them. Fighting broke out. Eventually in 1783- Britain recognized the colonies independence.

War with France

Napoleon was Emperor of France. British Navy beat the French and Spanish at the 'Battle of Trafalgar' in 1805. Admiral Nelson was killed in battle. Nelsons column is in Trafalgar square. His ship HMS victory can be seen at Portsmouth.

French wars ended in 1815. Duke of Wellington defeated Napoleon at battle of Waterloo and was known as 'Iron Duke'. He later became Prime Minister.

The Union Flag

Also known as the Union Jack. It is three crosses combined from England, Scotland and Ireland. There is also an official Welsh flag- but doesn't not appear in union jack as Wales was United with England when the union jack was created in 1606.

Victorian age

1837 Queen Victoria is Queen at 18. She was the longest reigning monarch. Her time is known as Victorian age, when Britain increased power and influence abroad.

British Empire

British Empire grew to cover all of India, Australia and parts of Africa. People left to go overseas and some came to Britain.
Russian and polish Jews came to escape persecution. People from India and Africa came to Britain to live work and study.

Trade and Industry

Britain continued to be a great trading nation. Free trade was promoted and taxes on imports of items were removed. One example is the Corn Laws in 1846.

Working conditions improved. Hours of work for women and children were limited by law to 10 hours per day.

Transport links improved. George and Robert Stephenson pioneered railway engines.
Bridge building also advanced. Isambard Kingdom Brunel was an

engineer. He built the great western railway. Many of Brunel's bridges are still in use.

1851: Great Exhibition opens in Hyde Park at Crystal Palace. This building was made of steel and glass. Most objects on show were British made.

Crimean war

First war to be extensively covered by media (newspapers, photography). Conditions were poor and many soldiers died due to infections in hospitals.

Florence Nightingale

She was a nurse who improved hospital conditions and so reduced the death rate in hospitals.

Ireland-potato famine

Many people depended on potatoes for their diet. When the potato crop failed, many died. A lot of Irish people left. Some went to United States, others to England and settled in Manchester Liverpool, London Glasgow.

Right to vote

The Reform act of 1832 meant that increased numbers of people could vote. There was a shift of power from the countryside to towns, but was still based on ownership of property.

A group known as chartists began to demand votes for working class. 1867: a reform act reduced the amount of property needed to vote.

Emmeline Pankhurst

She was part of a group called suffragettes. They tried to get voting rights for women.

1882 – Women have the right to own earnings, property and money.

1918 - Women over 30 can vote.

1928 - Women over 21 can vote.

1960s, 1970s - Parliament passed laws prohibiting discrimination, and giving equal pay.

Future of the empire

Questions were being asked by many over whether the Empire might be over expanding, and draining resources. Boer war in Africa was between Britain and settlers in South Africa who wanted independence. Slowly different parts of the British Empire started to become independent.

Rudyard Kipling. Born in India. Believed Empire was a good thing. Wrote 'Jungle Book' and 'Just so' stories. Won Nobel prize 1907.

First world war- 1914

Centred in Europe, but was a global war. The whole of the British Empire was involved. Ended 11th November, at 11am IN 1918. Britain and its allies had won.

Partition of Ireland

1922: Ireland became two countries. Northern Ireland and Ireland. Many people disagreed with the split.

17

Inter war period

1920's living conditions got better.

Housing improved, new houses built.

But in 1929: 'Great depression' happened. There was mass unemployment. Prices fell and people in work could buy more. Car ownership doubled.

Second World War

War was between Axis powers (Germany Italy Japan).

Adolf Hitler was leader of Germany and invaded Poland.

Germany bombed cities in Britain. This was called the 'blitz'. Coventry was almost destroyed. 'Blitz spirit': means coming together to face adversity.

Dunkirk Spirit: British and French soldiers escaped to the beach around Dunkirk. Volunteers in small fishing boats rescued them. This is called the 'Dunkirk Spirit'.

Winston Churchill was a solider and journalist and became Prime Minister in 1940. He was an inspirational leader.

2002: he was voted greatest Briton of all time by the public.

He made famous speeches such as: 'we shall fight them on the beaches' and 'I have nothing to offer but blood toil tears and sweat.'

United States entered the war when Japan bombed Pearl Harbour.

6th June 1944 is called D-day, when allied forces landed on beach of Normandy.

War with Japan ended 1945- because United States dropped atomic bombs on two Japan cities: Hiroshima and Nagasaki.

War was over.

Alexander Fleming discovered Penicillin. He won Nobel Prize for medicine.

Britain since 1945

1945 the Labour Party came to power. Led by Clement Atlee.

NHS was established (free healthcare for everyone).

Government took ownership (nationalized) gas supply, electric supply, coal mines, and trains.

1947: independence granted to nine countries including India, Pakistan, Ceylon (Sri Lanka), later to parts of Africa, Caribbean and pacific.

Britain developed atomic bomb and joined NATO. This was an alliance of nations to resist threat of Soviet Union.

R. A. Butler: Conservative MP. Introduced the Education Act (also called Butler act). This provided free secondary school education for all.

Dylan Thomas: Welsh poet and writer. He read and performed in public. Died age 39. Famous poem 'Go gentle into the good night'. His statue is in Swansea at the Dylan Thomas Centre.

Migration in post-war Britain

After World War 2, Irish and Europeans were encouraged to come to the UK to help with the reconstruction.

1950s - shortage of labour. Migrants from West Indies, India and

Pakistan came to work. They worked as Bus drivers, Taxi drivers, in textile industry, engineering industries, food production.

Social change in 1960s

This is known as the 'swinging sixties', because of a growth in fashion, cinema, music. Two famous pop-groups were the 'Beatles', and the 'Rolling Stones'.

Some laws were liberalized, for example divorce and abortion.

1970s - more restrictions place in labour migrants. Increasing refugees from Uganda, Vietnam and S.E. Asia.

1980s - immigration mainly from US, Australia, South Africa and New Zealand.

1990s - increasing political and economic migration from former Soviet Union.

Some great British inventions of 20th century

John Logie Baird= Television
Sir Robert Watson-Watt= Radar
Sir Bernard Lovell with Robert= radio telescope at Jodrell Bank in Cheshire
Alan Turing= Turing machine (influenced modern day computers)
John Macleod=Insulin for diabetes
Francis Crick= structure of DNA
Sir Frank Whittle= jet engine
Sir Christopher Cockerell =hovercraft
Harrier Jump Jet- developed in UK
James Goodfellow=cash machine- ATM
Sir Robert Edwards & Patrick Steptoe- IVF

Cloning= British scientist

Sir Peter Mansfield=MRI

Sir Tim Berners-Lee= World Wide World

Problems with the Economy: 1970s

Prices for goods and materials went high. Many strikes occurred. There was conflict between Trade Unions and government.

In Northern Ireland Parliament was suspended and was ruled by UK government.

Mary Peters

Moved to Northern Ireland when a child. Won Olympic gold medal pentathlon in 1972. She did a lot of work to raise money for the women's Olympic British team. In 2000 - made Dame of the British Empire.

Europe and common market

EEC: West Germany, France, Belgium, Italy, Luxembourg, Netherlands. 1957.

1973: UK joined EEC. We are full member but do not use Euro currency.

Conservative government 1979-1997

Margaret Thatcher was a chemist and lawyer. First woman Prime minister for UK. She made changes to economy. Privatized many industries.

Argentina invaded Falkland Islands.

John Major was Prime Minister after Thatcher. He helped establish the Northern Island peace process.

Roald Dahl- a writer. Wrote many children's books such as 'Charlie and the chocolate factory', 'George Marvellous Medicine'.

Labour Government 1997-2010

Tony Blair elected 1997.

Introduced Welsh assembly and Scottish parliament.

Northern Island: Blair built upon the peace process Good Friday Agreement signed 1998.

Conflict Afghanistan and Iraq

Britain played a major role in the coalition to liberate Kuwait when Iraq invaded it. UK is part of the United Nations and operates in Afghanistan.

Coalition Government

May 2010: no party won overall majority in the election.

Conservative and Liberal Democrat parties formed coalition- David Cameron became Prime Minister.

Chapter 2:
A modern, thriving society

The UK today
Longest distance on the mainland is from John O' Groats to Lands End in Scotland.

Capital cities
England=London
Wales=Cardiff
Scotland=Edinburgh
Northern Island=Belfast

UK Currency
Coins: 1p 5p 10p 20p 50p £1 £2
Notes: £5 £10 £20 £50

Languages & dialects
Wales= Welsh- taught in schools and universities
Scotland=Gaelic spoken in some parts of Highlands and Islands
Northern Ireland= some people speak Irish Gaelic

UK Population=just over 62 million
Growth faster in recent years due to Migration into UK and long life expectancy.

Aging population: UK people are living longer because: living standards have improved and there is better health care. There is a record number of people aged over 65.

Ethnic diversity

UK population is ethnically diverse. Especially in large cities in London and Birmingham.

Equal society

Within the UK everyone has the right to work, own property marry or divorce.

Women make up about half of the workforce.
On average girls leave school with better qualifications than boys. More women than men study at university.

No longer expected that women should stay home and not work.

Religion

Everyone has the right to choose their religion, or choose not to practice a religion.

Christian-70%
No religion 21%
Muslim 4%
Hindu 2%
Sikh 1%
Jewish & Buddhist -0.5%
Other %

Christian Churches

England: there is a constitutional link between Church and State. Official church is Church of England since reformation. In Scotland and United states it is called Episcopal Church.

Scotland: National church called Church of Scotland. It is Presbyterian.

There is no established church for Wales or Northern Island.
Other protestant Christian groups are Baptists, Methodists, Quakers, and Presbyterians. Finally is the Roman Catholic.

Patron Saints' Days of the four countries of the UK are:

- St David's Day, Wales – 1 March
- St Patrick's Day, Northern Ireland – 17 March
- St George's Day, England – 23 April
- St Andrew's day, Scotland – 30 November

Only Scotland and Northern Island have a patron saint as an official holiday. But in England and Wales we celebrate with parades.

Customs and traditions

Christmas Day 25th December. Trees are decorated. Special meal eaten which includes turkey, mince pies and Christmas pudding. Children believe in Father Christmas (Santa Claus) who gives presents during the night before Christmas day.

Boxing Day 26th: public holiday

Easter: 40 days before Easter is known as Lent. Traditionally (in the past) people would fast, today they give something up. Day before Lent is known as Shrove Tuesday or Pancake Day. Next day is Ash Wednesday. There are church services and Christians are marked with an ash cross.

Easter is celebrated by everyone. Easter eggs are given as presents and are a symbol of new life.

Diwali- October/November- lasts five days. Called festival of lights. Celebrated by Sikhs and Hindus. Celebrates victory of good over evil.

Hanukkah: November/December. Eight days. Candle lit each day (a menorah). It remembers Jews struggle for freedom.

Eid-al-fitr: End of Ramadan after Muslims have fasted one month.

Eid ul Adha: Muslims sacrifice an animal to eat. In Britain the animal is killed in slaughterhouse. They remember Prophet Ibrahim who was asked by God to sacrifice his son.

Vaisakhi: 14th April. Celebrates founding of Sikh community (khalsa). There are parades, dancing and singing.

Other festivals and traditions

New Year's Day– 1 January. People celebrate on New Year's Eve (Scotland called Hogmanay- for some this is bigger than Christmas.). In Scotland 2nd January is also Public holiday.

Valentine's Day – 14 February. Lovers exchange cards

April fool's Day – 1 April. Lasts until midday. People play jokes.

Mothering Sunday: Three weeks before Easter. Children buy gifts and give cards to mother.

Father's day: 3rd Sunday in June. Children give cards or gifts to father.

Halloween: 31 October. Young dress up in scary costumes to play trick or treat. They knock doors and people give treats stop the children playing a 'trick'.

Guy Fawkes Night: 5 November – also called bonfire night. Fireworks. This celebrates the failure of Guy Fawkes & others to blow up King and Houses of Parliament.

Remembrance Day: 11am on 11 November. Remember the dead who died in First World War. 2 minute silence at 11am, and wreaths laid at cenotaph in Whitehall London.

Bank holidays: a public holiday when banks other businesses are closed. Two in May, one in June one in August. Northern Island-also one in July to celebrate battle of Boyne.

Sport

Sports and sporting events which are popular in the UK

Football
Rugby
Tennis
Cricket
Grand National Horse Race
FA Cup Final
Open Golf Championship
Wimbledon Tennis Tournament

UK has hosted Olympic Games three times. Last time was in 2012 in London.

Paralympic games-hosted in London 2012. For people with physical disability.

Cricket

These words are associated with cricket:

Rain stopped play

Batting on sticky wicket

Playing a bat

Bowled a googly

It's just not cricket

Most famous competition is called 'The Ashes' between England and Australia.

Football

UK's most popular sport. England, Scotland wales and northern have each have leagues. English premier league attracts an international audience. Best players in the world play in this league.

Each country in the UK has its own national team who play in world tournaments. Example FIFA, world cup, and UEFA.

Rugby

Two types of rugby.

Union and league.

Most famous rugby union is the six nation's championship.

Super league is the most well-known rugby league.

Horse racing

Famous horse racing events are:

Royal Ascot attending royal family.

Grand National at Liverpool. Scottish Grand National. There is a horse racing museum in new market Suffolk.

Golf

St Andrews in Scotland is known as home of golf.

Tennis

Most famous is the Wimbledon. Championships. Every year. The only grand slam played on grass.

Water sports

Sir Francis Chichester was the first person to sail by himself around the world in 1966/67. Sir Robin Knox-Johnson did the same without stopping.

Motor sports

Includes car and motorcycle. Formula 1 grand prix held in UK every year. A number of British drivers have won formula 1. Damon Hill, Lewis Hamilton, Jenson Button.

Skiing

Many go abroad to ski. Five ski centres in Scotland's and Europe's longest dry ski slope is in Edinburgh.

Arts and culture

Music

There are many different venues and musical events that take place in UK.

The proms: 8 week summer season of orchestral classical music. Takes places in many venues including Royal Albert Hall in London.
The Last Night of the Proms: well known concert that comes on television.

Henry Purcell: was organist at Westminster Abbey. Wrote church music and operas.

George Frederick Handel: German but became British citizen. Wrote Water Music for King George I. Music for the Royal Fireworks for King George II.

Gustav Holst: wrote the Planets.

Sir Edward Elgar: wrote March No 1 (Land of hope and glory) is played at Last Night of the Proms at Royal Albert Hall.

Ralph Vaughan Williams: Music for orchestra and choirs.

Sir William Walton: wrote marches for the coronations of King George and Elizabeth II.

Benjamin Britten: wrote operas, famous are Peter Grimes and Billy Budd.

Music event venues are: Wembley stadium, O2 arena in Greenwich, Scottish exhibition & conference centre in Glasgow.

Festival season takes place in summer-they include Glastonbury festival, Isle of wright festival, and V festival.

National Eisteddfod of Wales: annual festival music, dance, art, poetry competitions

Mercury music prize: for best album. Brit award- best British group and artist prize.

Theatre

London West End is known as Theatre land. The Mousetrap by Dame

Agatha Christie has had the longest run of any show in history.

Gilbert and Sullivan wrote comic operas. These include HMS Pinafore, Pirates of Penzance, and The Mikador.

Andrew Lloyd Weber has written music for shows popular throughout the world, example: Cats, Evita, phantom of the opera and Jesus Christ superstar.

Pantomimes are popular at Christmas. These are family comedy shows based on fairy tales.

Edinburgh festival: every summer a series of art and cultural festivals. Biggest is known as 'The Fringe', which are theatre and comedy performances.

Laurence Olivia Awards: every year in London. Awards for best actor, actress and director. Laurence was a British actor who used to play roles in Shakespeare.

Art
Well known art galleries are The National Gallery, Tate Britain, Tate Modern, National museum in Cardiff, National gallery of Scotland in Edinburgh.

Turner Prize: 4 works are chosen every year and shown at Tate Britain. One winner is announced. Previous winners: Damien Hirst and Richard Wright.

Architecture
Early times- great cathedrals and churches were built such as Durham, Canterbury, and Lincoln ad Salisbury.

White tower in tower of London is example of a Norman castle keep built by William conqueror. Inigo Jones designed Queen's house in Greenwich and banqueting house in Whitehall.

Christopher Wren built new St. Paul's cathedral (after great fire destroyed the old one).

Dumfries house Scotland: designed by Robert Adam.

19th century: Gothic style was popular. Examples are House of parliament, St. Pancreas station and town halls in some cities like Manchester.

20th century: Sir Edwin Lutyen. Designed New Delhi to be seat of government in India. After war built war memorials such as the cenotaph in London.

Garden design also had an important role in UK. 18th century Lancelot 'capability' Brown designed grounds around country houses.

Chelsea flower show: showcases garden design from Britain and around the world.

Fashion and design
Britain has produced many great designers such as:

Thomas Chippendale (furniture), Clarice Cliff (art deco ceramics). Fashion designers Alexander McQueen, Vivian Westwood.

Literature
Several British writers have won Novel prizes for literature: Harold Pinter, Sir William Golding, Seamus Heaney.

Others have become well known- Agatha Christie=crime novels, Ian Fleming=James Bond.

JRR Tolkien wrote Lord of the Rings was voted country best loved novel.

Man Booker Prize: annual prize for best fiction for writer from commonwealth, Ireland or Zimbabwe. Winners include Ian McEwan, Hilary Mantel and Julian Barnes.

British Poets

Britain has a very rich history of poetry.

Anglo-Saxon poem Beowulf is still translated today.

Middle ages: Chaucer's Canterbury tales, Sir Gawain and Green Knight.

Others: Shakespeare, William Wordsworth

19th century: William Blake, John Keats, Percy Shelly.

Leisure

Gardening. Many people enjoy gardening. People sometimes rent plots called allotments to grow fruit and vegetables.

Gardens to visit: Kew Gardens, Sissinghurst and Hidcote. Crathes castle and Inveraray castle Scotland. Bodnant garden Wales, and Mount Stewart in Ireland.

Flowers associated with countries of the UK:
England-rose, Scotland-Thistle, Wales-daffodil, Northern Island-shamrock.

Shopping: Most shops open seven days a week. But trading hours on Sunday and public holidays reduced.

Cooking and food: Many people enjoy cooking.

Traditional foods:

England: Roast beef. Yorkshire pudding, fish and chips.

Wales: Welsh cakes.

Scotland: Haggis —stuffed sheep's stomach.

Northern Ireland: Ulster fry. Fried meal bacon eggs, sausage black pudding.

Films

Sir Charlie Chaplin was a British actor who worked in silent movies and famous in Hollywood.

Directors such as Alfred Hitchcock left for Hollywood and became famous.

Second World War British movies helped to boost morale.

1950's/60's —was a high point for comedy film.

Harry Potter and James Bond have been made in the UK.

Ealing studios is oldest working film studio in the world.

Nick Park won Oscars for Wallace and Gromit for animated films.

British actors have won Oscars including Colin firth, Kate Winslet, Tilda Swinton, Dame Judi Dench.

British Academy film awards: British equivalent of the Oscars.

Some famous British films
Chariots of fire
Killing fields
Four weddings and funeral

British comedy
Comedy has been a popular part of British culture.

Television and radio
A Television License is a Legal requirement for watching television. It is used to pay for Public service television (the BBC). Over 75's-can get a free license. Blind get 50% discount. £1000 fine for not having license.

Social networking
Twitter and Facebook are a way for people to keep in touch with friends and family and others.

Pubs and night clubs
A pub is a public house. A place to buy alcohol and sit and watch television, play snooker or darts. Must be 18 to buy alcohol. Age 16 you can have drink with a meal if with someone over 18.

The owner decides opening hours of the pub/club. Usually open 11am and 12pm on Sundays.

Betting and gambling
Must be 18 to go into betting shop. 16 or over to buy lottery ticket.

Pets
Dogs must have collar and tag with owner's names and address when

at public places. Owner must keep dog under control and clean up after their dog messes in public places. Veterinary surgeons offer medicine and medical help.

Places of interest

There are 15 national parks in England wales and Scotland.

Many parks and places of interested looked after by National Trust (a charity).

Big ben- London clock over 150 years old. Also known as Elizabeth Tower.

Other places of interest:

Eden project- Cornwall.
Edinburgh castle- Scotland.
Giants causeway- North east coast Northern Ireland.
Loch Lomond at Trossachs national park- Scotland.
London Eye, Tower of London- London.
Snowdonia - Wales.
Lake District- England's largest National Park. Biggest stretch of water is Lake Windermere.

Chapter 3: UK Government- law and your role

Development of British democracy

UK has a constitutional democracy. This is where all of the adult population has a say.

British constitution

Head of State= Monarch. Opens each session of Parliament. Closes (dissolves) Parliament before a general election. Approves Orders and Proclamations.

National Anthem of UK is: 'God Save the Queen'. Sung at important occasions or events.

Citizenship ceremony –people are asked to swear loyalty to the Queen as part of the ceremony.

System of Government

House of Commons

Made up of Members of Parliament, elected by the public during general elections to represent constituencies (small areas of the country).

Commons are important: create new laws, scrutinize what the Government is doing (the opposition does this), and debate important issues.

House of Lords

It is Parliament's Second House or Chamber. The Lords, also known as Peers, are not elected and do not represent constituencies. Its members are Life Peers appointed by the Monarch (Queen).

They are

- Hereditary Peers,
- Senior Judges,
- Church of England Bishops,
- Appointed Life Peers.

The speaker: chairs and keeps order during debates in the House of Commons. He is neutral.

Elections: Take place least every 5 years. Government is formed by the party with the largest number of MPs. The system is First past the post. Candidate with the most vote wins.

The public can contact elected members: by telephone or letter. Or meeting at surgeries held at places like libraries, schools, or community centres.

Prime Minister is an MP. He is selected by the party to be the leader. When his Party wins he becomes Prime Minister. He/she appoints the members of the Cabinet (also from his own party) and has control over many important public appointments.

The cabinet: advises the Prime Minister. They have different roles in the Cabinet for example:

- Prime Minister
- First Lord of the Treasury
- Minister for the Civil Service
- Deputy Prime Minister
- Lord President of the Council
- First Secretary of State
- Secretary of State for Foreign and Commonwealth Affairs
- Chancellor of the Exchequer
- Lord Chancellor
- Secretary of State for Justice
- Secretary of State for the Home Department
- Minister for Women and Equality
- Secretary of State for Defence
- Secretary of State for Business, Innovation and Skills
- Secretary of State for Work and Pensions
- Secretary of State for Energy and Climate Change
- Secretary of State for Health
- Secretary of State for Education
- Secretary of State for Communities and Local Government
- Secretary of State for Transport
- Secretary of State for Environment, Food and Rural Affairs
- Secretary of State for International Development
- Secretary of State for Northern Ireland
- Secretary of State for Scotland
- Secretary of State for Wales

- Secretary of State for Culture, Olympics, Media and Sport
- Chief Secretary to the Treasury
- Leader of the House of Lords
- Chancellor of the Duchy of Lancaster
- Minister for the Cabinet Office
- General Paymaster

The Opposition: Second largest party in the House of Commons. The role of the Leader of the Opposition is to lead in holding the government to account.

The Party System: Anyone over 18 can stand for election. But to represent one of the political parties you must be nominated by them to stand.

UK, Irish and Commonwealth citizens can stand. But not armed forces, civil servants and convicted criminals.

Civil service: Civil servants carry out government policies. Politically neutral but advises or warns if government policies are not practical.

Local Government

Towns, cities and rural areas are governed by elected council. Also called local authorities.
They provide services in their area. Some authorities appoint a mayor. Local elections for councillors are held in May every year.

Devolved administrations: this is where power over certain areas given over.

Welsh Assembly has these powers:

- Agriculture, fisheries, forestry and rural development
- Ancient monuments and historic buildings
- Culture
- Economic development
- Education and training
- Environment
- Fire and rescue services and promotion of fire safety
- Food
- Health and health services
- Highways and transport
- Housing
- Local government
- Public administration
- Social welfare
- Sport and recreation
- Tourism
- Town and country planning
- Water and flood defence
- Welsh language

Scottish Parliament has these powers:

- Agriculture,
- Fisheries
- Forestry
- Economic Development
- Education
- Environment
- Food Standards
- Health
- Home Affairs
- Courts

- Police
- Fire Services
- Local Government
- Sport
- The Arts
- Transport
- Training
- Tourism
- Research
- Statistics
- Social Work
- Civil and Criminal Law
- Additional Taxes

The Scottish Parliament also has the ability to alter income tax in Scotland by up to 3 pence in the pound.

Northern Ireland Assembly has these powers:

- Enterprise, Trade and Investment
- Finance & Personnel
- Regional Development
- Education
- Employment and Learning
- Environment
- Culture, Arts & Leisure
- Health,
- Social Services
- Public Safety
- Agriculture and Rural Development
- Social Development
- Justice

These areas of policy remain under the control of the UK Government: Policy, defence, foreign affairs, taxation, and social security.

Proportional representation: used in the Scottish Parliamentary, Welsh Assembly and Northern Irish Assembly elections.

Parties get the number of seats in proportion to the number of votes they receive.

Media and Government

Proceedings in parliament are shown on television and printed in 'The Hansard'.

UK has a free press: Government has no control over newspapers or television. By law- radio and television covering political news must be balanced (given equal time).

Voting- who can vote?

All UK citizens over 18.
Commonwealth citizens.
Irish Republic citizens resident in UK.
EU citizens resident in UK can vote in all except parliamentary elections.

All of the above can vote at 18 years old except for convicted criminals in prison.

To vote: you must register on the local Electoral Register. It is updated every year and local authority must make it available for viewing by public.

Voting is done at polling stations- these can be setup in schools. A card is sent to voters showing where they must go to vote.

Visiting:

To visit UK Parliament you can write to your MP for tickets. Or queue at entrance.

Visit Northern Island Assembly: contact education, or contact MLA.

Visit Scottish Parliament: Book tickets or tour through visitor service.

National Assembly Wales- book tour or seat in public gallery contact Assembly booking service.

The UK and International institutions

The Commonwealth is an association of 53 countries which were once part of the British Empire.

The European Union (EU): Union of some European countries

Council of Europe: is separate from EU: It has 47 countries and tries to promote human rights. It does not make laws.

The EU Commission is the civil service drafts proposals and administers funding programs. EU law is legally binding in all member states.

The EU Parliament provides checks and balances against the Council and Commission.

United Nations: 190 countries as members to promote international peace and security. 15 members on UN Security Council which takes actions.

NATO: Group of Europe countries and North America countries which agree to help each other if ever attacked.

Respecting the law

Everyone receives equal treatment under UK law.

There are two parts to law:

Criminal law: people who are charged with crimes such as murder, assault, robbery.

Civil law which are used to settle disputes between individuals or groups such as in divorce cases, debt problems, housing law.

The Police and their duties

Police: are organized locally for each area. They prevent and detect crime, protect people and property, prevent disturbances-keep peace. They themselves must obey the law.

PCSO's =Police community support officer-support police officers.

In 2012: people elected police and crime commissioners. They are responsible for delivery of policing, set local priority local budget and appoint chief constable.

If something goes wrong you can complain by going to police station or writing to chief constable. You can also contact the Independent Police complaints commission.

Terrorism and extremism: UK faces threats of extremist acts from terrorist and also dangers of people in the UK becoming radicalised and causing a danger.

The Role of the Courts

The Judiciary: Judges interpret the law. Government cannot interfere with them. If it is claimed that the government is not following law and if judges agree then parliament has to change its law or policies.

Criminal courts:

Youth court: Crimes committed by 10-17 years old. Closed court (no public allowed). Serious cases go straight to crown court.

Magistrates court (Peace court in Scotland): minor criminal cases.

Crown court-(Sheriff Court in Scotland): most serious cases.

High court (only in Scotland) –very serious cases like murder.

Juries in England wales and NI: 12 people. Verdict can be guilty or not guilty.

Juries in Scotland: 15 people. Verdict is guilty, not guilty, and not proven.

Civil courts

County court: deals with these cases.

In Scotland most serious civil case will go to sheriff court (high monetary compensations).

Small claims procedure: for claims of less than £5000 or £3000 in Scotland. Fast way to settle minor problems without need for lawyer.

Legal advice

Solicitor: are trained lawyers who give legal advice. They will specialize in certain areas. Find one from yellow pages, newspapers, or law society.

Fundamental principles

Rights that people have their roots in the Magna Carta, habeas corpus act and bill of rights.

The citizenship ceremony: new citizens pledge to uphold values

UK helped with creating the European convention on human rights. The human rights act 1998 meant that these human rights were added to UK law. Public bodies and courts must follow these principles. These include:

Right to life
Prohibition of torture, slavery, forced labour
Right to fair trial
Freedom of thought, speech, expression, religion, conscience

Equal opportunities

UK Laws ensure that no one is treated unfairly because of age, sex, disability, race, religion, maternity, sexuality, belief marital status.

Domestic violence: Violence in the home is a serious crime. Anyone who is violent against the partner (man or woman) can be prosecuted.

A man who forces a woman to have sex (including the husband) can be charged with rape.

Some places have safe areas called refuges or shelters to go and stay. You can phone a free 24 hour help line for help.

Female genital mutilation: this is cutting or circumcision of female private parts. Illegal in UK as is taking a girl abroad for FGM.

Forced Marriage: in UK both parties must agree to marry.

2007: Forced marriage act: court orders can be obtained to protect anyone from being forced to marry. The victim or anyone acting for them can apply for court order.

Taxation

Income tax: paid by all who work for others or are self-employed. Income from savings interest, pension are also taxed.

Most people collected automatically by a system called PAYE (pay as you earn). The money is collected by HMRC (Her Majesty's Revenue and Customs).

Self-employed people: pay via a system called 'self-assessment'. They complete a tax return form.

Income Tax money is used for services such as roads, education, police and armed forces.

National insurance

Everyone in paid work or self-employed pay this. It is used for state benefits such as pension and National Health Service (NHS).

All young people at 16 are given a National Insurance number which tracks payments made. You can start work without a number but will need to apply for one.

Driving

17 to drive a car. License: Apply for provisional license, pass written theory test, pass practical driving test.

.

EU license can be used for as long as it is valid. Other driving licences can be used for one year.

Cars must be registered to the driver and must pay annual car tax. Owners must also have car insurance.

MOT: is a test of the car for road worthiness. All cars over 3 years must have this done every year.

Your role in the community

Everyone in the UK has the right to participate in the community. There are shared values and responsibilities which include

-Obey the law
-Treat others with fairness
-Help others
-Respect and preserve the environment
-Be a good neighbour: they are a good source of help. You can prevent problems by respecting privacy and how much noise you make.

Supporting community

Jury service: People 18-70 on the electoral register can be randomly selected to serve on a jury

Helping in schools: parents can help in schools by supporting activities. Some schools raise money for equipment and need help to run events to raise money. Sometimes parent-teacher associations will help to organize the event (PTA)

School governor: are people from the local community. Their role is to ensure accountability, monitor school performance, and set strategic direction for school. You can ask the school if they need a governor.

Political parties

You can support by joining a party whose views you support. At election time you can help by handing leaflets out or knocking doors asking for support.

You can also stand for election as a councillor, Member of Parliament or member of European Parliament.

Helping with local services

You can help at many places such and in many projects such as youth projects. You can volunteer with police as special constable. You can apply to be a magistrate.

Volunteering

Volunteering is a good way to improve your CV, and help when finding a job as it gives you experience. There are many charities and volunteering organization in the UK where you can volunteer.

Age UK- helps older people
Crisis/ Shelter: helps homeless (shelter helps those fleeing domestic violence
NSPCC- children charity

For young people 16-17: there is national citizenship programme.

Blood & Organ donation

Giving blood takes one hour. Many people are waiting for organ transplants. You can register to be an organ donor to make it easier for your family to make a decision when you die.

Looking after environment

Recycling: you should recycle as much as you can. Making new products from recycled materials uses less energy, and raw materials do not have be extracted from the earth.

Less rubbish is created by recycling, so less amount is added to landfill (place where rubbish is put).

Shopping locally helps local businesses and farmers in your area. It reduces carbon footprint as you do not travel far.

Walking is good for health and so is using public transport. It protects the environment as you create less pollution if you do not use your car.

Some tips when taking the test

Booking the test: ensure you enter your ID details exactly as it appears, as this will be checked for an exact match at the test centre. Many people are refused entry to the test when ID details have not matched the details entered when booking the test.

Breakfast: your brain needs energy to work efficiently. Ensure you have a good breakfast (or lunch if appropriate) on the day of the test.

Read questions twice: make sure you read each question at least two times before you pick an answer. A common mistake is picking an answer to a question which you think is being asked, rather than what is actually being asked.

Skip: go to the next question if you are unable to answer it or are unsure. You may find that other questions actually help you to answer the skipped question, or that your brain finds the answer after giving it time to think in the background.

Don't rush: you have 45 minutes to take the test. Make sure you use the full time given even if you finish early by going over your answers. You may discover that you had incorrectly answered a question and will be able to correct it.

30212319R00037

Printed in Great Britain
by Amazon

Charles Seale-Hayne Library
University of Plymouth
(01752) 588 588
LibraryandITenquiries@plymouth.ac.uk

FLUIDS AND PERIODIC STRUCTURES

OTHER TITLES IN THE SAME SERIES

INTERACTIONS FLUIDES-STRUCTURES, by J.P. MORAND and R. OHAYON. 1993, 224 pages.

RECENT ADVANCES IN PARTIAL DIFFERENTIAL EQUATIONS, by M.A. HERRERO and E. ZUAZUA. 1994, 160 pages.

APPLICATIONS OF MULTIPLE SCALING IN MECHANICS. APPLICATIONS DES ÉCHELLES MULTIPLES EN MÉCANIQUE. International conference reports, École normale supérieure de paris, november 1986. Chaired by P.G. CIARLET and E. SANCHEZ-PALENCIA. 1987, 360 pages.

ANALYSIS OF THE K-EPSILON. TURBULENCE MODEL, by B. MOHAMMADI and O. PIRONNEAU. 1994, 212 pages. Masson / John Wiley co-publication.

ÉCOULEMENTS DE FLUIDE : COMPACITÉ PAR ENTROPIE, by J. NECAS, notes taken by S. MAS-GALLIC. 1988, 112 pages.

NUMERICAL ANALYSIS OF VISCOELASTIC PROBLEMS, by P. LE TALLEC. 1990, 144 pages.